It was on a Christmas Day, when Flossie appeared in the desert, on the beam of a rainbow. Splashing in a swimming pool, to find Paul crying.

"Who are you?"
He said. "Flossie! The Christmas Mermaid", she replied. She was dressed in red and white.

She had a gold glittering tail and long blonde hair. There was a wiggle in her tail, and a jingle sound.

"Why are you crying Paul?" She said. "How come you know my name? Where do you come from?" Asked Paul. "I come from the bottom of the ocean where the rainbows are made."

"I saw you looking down in the pool and wishing so hard for happiness, it gave me a chill. So I got on a rainbow and here I am. Now Paul! Why are you so sad?"

"It's my mean stepmother, big Pearl," he sobbed. "She said, that Santa won't bring me any presents because the sun is so hot and there is no snow."

"What a cruel thing to say" cried Flossie the mermaid. "She must be a mean person." "Oh! She is! She is! She makes me sleep in the truck in the garage, a coat for a blanket, a tire tube for a pillow."

How cruel" said Flossie. "Don't worry Paul, there is a way." She had a mysterious smile. Paul stopped crying. Wondering what she meant.

Paul used to be happy before big Pearl moved in with her five sons.

Big Pearl was mean! She made Paul eat only leftovers. There was not even enough to feed a lizard.

Her sons had no respect for food. They over filled there glasses, and big Pearl yelled at Paul to clean up their messes.

Paul fell down on his knees! Flossie said, "All good things come to those who wait. Its never too late. I'll make your dream come true Paul."

Flossie swung her magic wand and wiggled her tail. Jingle! Jingle! She changed the cactus into christmas trees, and enchanted snow appeared.

Flossie and Paul built a snowman, made snow balls, and rolled in the snow. Oh! What fun they had.

She wiggled her tail again. Jingle! Jingle! The snow fell harder and harder until the desert was the prettiest christmas scene you ever saw.

They skied and skated down the hill, that minutes before had been nothing but hot dusty sand.

Paul had so much fun and played so hard that he fell asleep early that night. The tire tube felt warm and cozy. It seemed to glow in the dark.

Flossie watched over him awaiting for one more miracle. Then! The door flew open! Paul awakened to find his dad, hiding his tears.

I love you, son! He said, "Big Pearl will not be mean to you again." She moved out.

Paul was so happy! He smiled and said, "Flossie the sweet little mermaid made my dream come true.

Flossie slowly disappeared into thin air with the rainbow, like a mirage. The end.

Story written by:

Flossie Langdon Ward

Illustrated by:

Flossie Langdon Ward

COPYRIGHT 2013

A note about the author and illustrator,

Flossie Langdon Ward has dedicated her works to the love of Jesus, family and friends. She hopes you will enjoy for it is all in the name of the Lord.

Published by:

Flossie Langdon Ward

and

Createspace Inc.

ISBN13: 9780692504130 (Flossie Ward)
ISBN10: 0692504133

www.ingramcontent.com/pod-product-compliance
Lightning Source LLC
Chambersburg PA
CBHW041552220426
43666CB00002B/51